A BETTER UNDERSTANDING

OF LIFE'S JOURNEYS

IN BLACK & WHITE

A Memoria by

DEBORAH JETER

Designed by Deborah Jeter

I dedicate this book to my family and friends. May it give you incite and wisdom to succeed in whatever life throws at you.

As this book is just the beginning, I hope and pray that it will give the readers some strength and courage to boldly face life's challenges! May this inspire you and help you understand. Everyone is different in our own way and to accept a person for their uniqueness. May it help you to find your place in today's world!

Contents

A BETTER UNDERSTANDING

OF LIFE'S JOURNEYS

IN BLACK & WHITE

Introduction

"Let us always meet each other with smile, for the smile is the beginning of love"   Mother Teresa

I was born with beautiful blue eyes, patiently waiting for what life had in store for me.

Throughout the years, I would develop my caring heart and my ability to strike up a conversation with anyone. To have empathy for what they were going through. I truly feel these abilities were developed through my life experiences. I survived life through my quest for knowledge and understanding. Understanding who I am and why. You cannot understand someone unless you walk in their shoes. I hope that I give you the knowledge and understanding to concur your own battles with life.

I have always been compassionate about helping people and animals. Both have been my life! I am very displeased at what is happening in the world today! Had it not been for some life changing events on my end, to be honest I probably would probably still be in my own little world. Now I have time to focus on real issues helping you. By helping you, I am also helping myself!

I started writing a book several months ago about Bear Path Acres. I realized I had more to offer. How could I write a book without you understanding who I was and why? What drives my compassion, what makes me the person that I am?

I quickly understood that in my experiences, I have the ability to help so many more people beyond the animal world! I was driven by a force to start at the beginning of my life's journeys. What a driving force it has been. Every morning I would wake up and pray "Lord what do you want me to work on today?"

For years, I have said I was going to write a book about my life's journeys, for years I have put it off. This time was so much different. The words just flew faster than I could type. Nothing like what was in my mind, nothing like I had planned to write.

If this book helps just one person, then it is well worth my time in writing it. May it give you a better understanding and knowledge you did not have before.

FROM MY HEART TO YOURS WITH MUCH LOVE AND CARING,

Deborah (Debbie) Jeter

1

Baby Boomer

I recently was at my families Thanksgiving Day gathering and I asked a simple question to two people. Both immediately reached for their phone to find the correct answer. Being the type of person that I am; I did my own research. Here is the results: baby boomers are categorized into 2 groups: Boomer 1 and Boomer 2. I might have been born into the Boomer 2 category, but that didn't seem to fit me. So I read more, I actually fit into the Boomer 1 generation, that didn't surprise me at all, it was something I already knew about myself. I didn't need someone writing about history to tell me what I actually lived. I am an Aquarius, which fits me to a tee. Looking back on life and what it has thrown me, I often wonder, how did I survive? I am told I am a "remarkable woman" but hasn't everybody been though trials and tribulations'? Or have I just had more than my fair share, you be the judge. +++ **1**.

When you are born, you inherit 50% of you mother's gene pool, and 50% of your father's gene pool. Therefore, each of us different. There were not enough studies completed to help us understand our gene pool. Today's world is much different! We now have the capability to fully understand which genes you inherited, concur those flaws and live a full happy life, but only if you choose to. Our genes determines all our human traits. It is our DNA that makes up our physical characteristics and also our behavioral characteristics, one of these genes is aggression. These genes where passed on to us by our parents.

My life has been a little crazy for use of a better word. Full of thrills and excitement, sorrow and pain, abuse, neglect, the list can go on! You get out of life what you put into it. I have tried to give it 110%, with much success and failure. What a learning experience it has been! I am going to share just a brief history, so brace yourself for the unknown. There is not a doubt in my mind this will help you overcome some of your own fears and obstacles. I want to take you, to a new level in your self-confidence. No matter what happens to you in life, you are a survivor! You can thrive and succeed in whatever life throws at you!

2

Mother

So where would you like for me to start? I am assuming a brief back ground is in order. My Mother was born in 1932, her birth name was Havanna Moon Askew. It is truly amazing how history repeats itself! Mother was one of five children. She grew up as a care giver to her siblings, as uncontrollable diabetes hit hard in the family tree. All four of her siblings died from diabetes related illnesses. She had to start working as a waitress at the age of 12 to help support the family. I spent so many hours and years listening to her stories (maybe my next book should be her and my Granny's stories?), all of which I treasure! Times were so different back then, just as they are today!

High School Graduation

3

Father

My Father was born in 1923, his birth name was Donald Humphrey. He came from not quite so a large family and they definitely were a little wealthier! They met when he was in Pipefitter's School, at what is now the Newport News Shipyard; to be honest the Shipyard's name has been changed, several times, so I might not have the "proper name of it for that time frame". It is high on my priority list to find out either. I refer to him as Humphrey quite often.

4

The Early Years

They married when Mother was just 15 years old. It was Mother's calgon take me away time, so she thought! The moved to Louisiana, she immediately got pregnant with my oldest sister; Frances (she was 11 years older than me), less than a year later came Jean (10 years older), six years later; Donna (four years older) and then me!

After my sister Jean was born they moved to Mexico, NY. That is when Mother really got bogged down, her calgon take me away days ended. Humphrey had a brother named Jack. Jack married Emma and they had children, I forget exactly how many they had. I remember at least 3 possibly more. Anyway, they liked their booze. So Mother ended up taking in and raising their children for a few years.

Another one of Humphrey's relatives also had three children by a first marriage and they were not taken care of so they also came to live with us. One of their names is Nancy. I say us lightly as I was not born yet. They continued to live with us until I was one and Mother moved back to Virginia leaving my father.

Looking back on it, as you know hind sight is always better. Mother having my sister; Donna, kept Nancy going. Donna became Nancy's baby!

So by the time I came around four years later, there wasn't enough time or energy, to take care of me. I know I was born with leg deformities; I had to wear braces on my legs at night to try and get them straight. I also had to wear my shoes on the opposite feet. To look at my legs today, it is very obvious, nothing lines up.

Humphrey always worked out of town and was gone Monday – Friday. He would also would be gone on Saturday, if he was fooling around with his mistress. Apparently he had one quite regularly. He was the "ladies man"! This left Mother at home taking care of all these children that wasn't hers plus the four that were hers. I can't imagine all the hard work. No electric washer or dryer, all of the meat was fresh and so was the vegetables from the garden. No going to Food Lion, Walmart, Farm Fresh or Kroger! Canning all those vegetables in the summer, washing all those clothes with a wringer washing machine. Plucking and cleaning all those chickens. This reminds me of a story.

It was a Sunday dinner, everyone was at the table eating and Humphrey asked Jean "Do you want a piece of" chicken? "You know why?" Hannah was Jean's pet chicken, that incident alone shows just how cold hearted he could be!

I was only one year old. Mother had enough and moved back home to Newport News, Va. Nancy came with us, the other two stayed in N.Y. This meant she was down to only 5 children!

5

Church Life

Now Mother said she was always very active in the church, in
N.Y. Moving to Virginia brought different challenges. Divorce was
not accepted in a southern Baptist church back then. Divorce
was a huge NO NO! I can't imagine how devastating that must
have been, to have to choose between a cheating husband and
the church you were raised in! Thank goodness times have
changed!

Even though Mother didn't go to church, that didn't mean that
we didn't. She made sure we were there every Sunday, for every
special day and for vacation bible school. She wanted to make
sure we knew who God was and to live and abide by his
principles. She also thought me that love makes allowances for
peoples weakness, something I never fully understood for many
years. I was truly blessed in all of her weakness to have such a
wonderful Mother, for none of us a perfect. We do not come
with instruction booklets to follow. We do the best we can, in
any given circumstance and hope we make the right choices,
sometimes we do sometimes we don't. We not put on this earth
to judge anybody unless of course you are a Judge. How can
you allow yourself to judge someone unless you have walked in
their shoes?

She took up bowling. The bowling alley was right across the
street from the apartments we lived in. She also took up dancing
and experiencing some freedom she had never known before.
Do you blame her, hell no!

Animals have always been in my blood!

6

First Memories

My first memories as a child are of my babysitter, Mrs. Couch. When the ice cream truck came she would get me an ice cream sandwich, I was allowed to eat the ice cream but the sandwich part I had to save for later. Explains why to this day, when I eat an ice cream sandwich I always eat the ice cream first!

Have you ever played barber shop or hair stylist as a child? I did! I cut my friend's long dark brown hair really short! I was still a very young age but boy that is one of those memories that doesn't go away. I don't remember getting into trouble. I just remember her Mother crying, so why is it such a vivid memory? I could see if I had been beaten, scolded, or something else but nothing! Just the memory of cutting her long beautiful hair!

7

New Additions

Then Mother got pregnant with my half-brother Ricky. Before I knew it I had a stepfather. His name was Harry.

Harry has quite a story behind him! He was originally from Wisconsin. When he was 12 years old his parents either traded him or sold him to a farmer to become a ranch hand. There he worked long and hard hours. When the Korean War started, he lied about his age and joined the Navy. His ship was stationed in Virginia where he met and married his first wife and they had 4 children. His wife liked to fool around finally he got tired of it, so they got divorced.

Harry bought a gas station on Jefferson Avenue. Back then they were called service stations; they filled the gas tank, checked the oil and cleaned the windshield! There was a gas war going on. Who could give the lowest prices. This is when he got out of business.

Harry was never afraid of hard work, but when he got home that was it. Don't expect him to cook, clean, take out the trash, etc... His sole job was to work and bring home his paycheck, period! A wife's job was to make dinner, fix his coffee, wash his clothes, do all the shopping, cleaning and take care of the children, even though Mother still worked! No equal rights there!

It is my opinion that the reason I grew up living in apartments is because you don't have to mow the grass or fix anything, they do it all for you.

Although, there is one year here and one year there, where they actually rented a house. The two times only lasted a year each.

8

First Secret Learned

I was recently talking to my sister and something that I had pushed in the back of my brain came forward. It is amazing how you try to lock the bad memories away so they do not hurt you anymore. The trouble with that is they can be unlocked at any time and if you haven't dealt those issues, they will kick you in the ass, as if they just happened. The secret I have found, is to talk about them. The more you talk about all the negatives in your life, the sooner they can turn into positives. They never go away but the hurt becomes bearable and does eventually go away.

9

Tunnel Vison

Back to story time: We were living in a rented house in the country. I was in either kindergarten or first grade (there was no pre K, back then) and just starting to learn how to read. Frances had already got married so that left Jean, Donna, Ricky and I. Mother always worked 2nd shift to cut out the expense of a babysitter. When Harry got home from work that was it, he was focused on the television only. I was trying to read my book and I asked him to help; bad mistake! After just a few minutes of my asking him what the words were, he started yelling "What are you stupid or something?" Of course I was stupid, I was just learning to read! Jean came to my rescue and jumped on Harry's back and they got into one hell of a fight! All because Harry's life was work and watch television. You see, you are able to cut up someone early in life by the hurtful words you use. Don't go through life cutting people up with these hurtful words. Your tongue is liked a fire, one spark can set a whole forest on fire. Probably from then on my forest was always on fire. I didn't know it then but Harry's hurtful words, had really cut me up on the inside. Something that affected me for many years. If you don't learn anything from this story then please learn this: You don't go through life cutting people up with your hurtful words!

With Harry having tunnel vison to the television I can only assume that is probably the reason why I have never been a big television watcher! To this day, it irritates me to no end to be around someone who is. If you want to pluck my nerves, turn on the television and become a couch potato. This is an everlasting effect from my childhood.

This was the last time Jean would come to my rescue in my childhood years. She got married and we moved back to the city, she stayed in the country and we grew further and further apart.

10

Love

You see Harry didn't know how to love. Love is something that is taught to us. When we are babies our Mothers would hold us, rock you and nurture you. This is how you learn love. Haven't you often wondered why we have to have "safe houses" for women to abandon their babies? The chances are extremely high that the very woman that abandoned her baby was not taught love. You see love is supposed to overlook a wrong but if you do not know how to love, then how do you know to overlook the wrong? I can only assume Harry's mother was not the nurturing type.

11

Respect

I was raised in a vanishing era. A time when we respected our elders, we never thought about or were allowed to question their actions. They earned our respect because we appreciated and learned from their past experiences. Something that I feel is lacking in the generations to follow. I was speaking to a much younger Preacher a few years ago and what he said about floored me. He said that respect was something that was earned. No one has ever taught me how to earn respect. How do you earn your children and Grandchildren's' respect? This concept totally blows my mind! I sure as hell don't understand it and to be quite frankly with you, I don't care to understand it. Call me old fashion but I am going to remind you that love is supposed to make allowances for people's weakness and we have been through enough hell on our own. If we, as elders have not earned your respect, then walk in our shoes for a few years.

All though life's journeys I never once questioned my Mother or ever doubted her love and devotion. I accepted her and loved her for being my Mother. There is not a single one of us that is perfect.

12

Family Genes

When we are born, we inherit genes from both of our parents. I inherited my intelligence and excellent memory from my father and my anxiety from my mother. For better or worst I had to learn to live with both. **+++2**

Both of my parents had a huge caring hearts. Humphrey would give you the shirt off his back. He would pick up hitch hikers and take them miles, even states out of his way just to take them where they were going.

Mother suffered from both depression and anxiety. I was very fortunate not to inherit the major depressive gene. One of my immediate family members was not. Therefore, I have spent a lifetime learning on ways to help. Through trial and error, I have found what works and what doesn't. **+++3**

I did inherit her anxiety gene. As a young child I can remember mother giving me her secret pills. Those secret pills were valium. Over the years, I have learned what sparks my anxiety and how not to trigger it. I am also prone to severe panic attacks. These panic attacks have triggers. I know exactly what will bring on a panic attack, so I totally avoid these situations. There has been many times I have left my shopping cart in the store to escape and prevent a panic attack. I have severe panic attacks at hospitals. This has led to numerous problems throughout my life. I am not going through that chapter in my life right now. It deserves a book by itself. That book will be ready in 2017, so be on the lookout!

By the time I came around all my sisters had tried everything under the sun and Mother always expected the worst. I was a good child, never got into trouble, a loner; never fitting in, an outcast; no one picked me for sports and such in school. I had one friend in Elementary school. She lived above me. Her name was Mary Ann. When Mary Ann moved I got another friend Dana; she was older than I was, by how much I don't remember but a few years.

13

Music

My life has been surrounded by music, I feel blessed for that. There isn't an occasion that goes by that I do not know a song for. During my younger years I thought that having older sisters was a curse and in a way as you read further it was, but now looking back, I find it a blessing, as I can remember so much more than other people my age because I lived it through my sisters! I cherish each and every memory.

Being the youngest I was exposed to so much! The music was fantastic, from Elvis Presley, The Beatles, The Rolling Stones (to be honest I have never cared about them and I still don't. Why listen to music if you cannot understand the words?), Jimi Hendrix, Janis Joblin, Johnny Cash, George Jones, Hank Williams, Sr. the list is never ending so it seems sometimes. What a remarkable time in history: make peace not war, burning your bras, the Peace rallies, the Vietnam War, the long haired hippy freaks, the protests, JFK being shot. I could go on forever I think!

14

Christmas

Since my life revolved around music, Christmas was a big one! Every year in July Mother would start playing Christmas songs. It would be many years before I found out the reason. In July, she would put our Christmas presents on layaway!

The one rule she pounded into my brain was "I'll be home for Christmas, you can count on me." It worked. I honestly cannot remember a year except those in upstate N.Y. that I was not home for Christmas! It didn't matter where I was, what was happening in my life, everything would have to wait. I had to be home for Christmas.

Christmas was mother's favorite time of year! This made it especially hard when she lost her eye sight. The last few years of her life was extremely hard on me. She would get so depressed and mad because she couldn't see good enough to do the things that she loved. Those few years of taking care of her and trying to accommodate her have left deep wounds on me. Wounds that one day I am hoping will heal.

15

Concerts

For the life of me, I cannot remember how old I was but I was a very young. There was a fine establishment named the "Bloody Bucket"; (I don't remember the real name but it was known for all the rowdy fights) Mother would take me there. Her and my Aunt Shirley danced all night long. After the bar closed at 2am, we would head to "The Blue Star Diner". There we would eat breakfast and get home somewhere around 4:00am. In today's world that would get you for child neglect but it was different back then.

She would also take me to concerts all the way in Norfolk. I am forever grateful for that because I met some really fantastic performers. One of them that really comes to my mind is Little Jimmie Dickens. I think he stands out so much because I was always going behind stage and he brought me out and talked to my Mother about it. The secret of getting behind stage was learned at an early age and something that I still used until my 50's. My whole life is filled with concerts and of course sneaking backstage to meet all the performers. I can't count how many performers I have met, it would take me to long to even try and sit here and remember.

So young and naïve.

16

Naive

Even though I was exposed to a lot I was still naive! I remember sitting on the back porch of the apartments (yes, I was raised in apartments) I couldn't have been but in maybe the 2ʳᵈ grade and one of the older kids came zooming by on his bicycle and asked me "do you hump for free" I had no idea what in the world he was referring to, my last name was Humphrey. It took me a few more years to fully understand it.

One trip really stays in my mind. We were visiting my Father in upstate N.Y. It was my sister; Frances, he boyfriend, Rocky, another one of their friends and me. I think what makes it so memorable is, that was the first time my Father got high! They were sitting around the table smoking a joint and Humphrey kept saying "I don't feel a thing" meanwhile all the kids including me was running around screaming and having a blast! He might not have felt anything but he sure was mellow!

Coming back home to Virginia: they were pulled over by a country cop! Luckily they had smoked their entire weed stash but the police officer sure did give them a lot of trouble for being long haired hippy freaks! He even went so far as to think that I was kidnapped! Eventually the police officer let us go and we were on our merry way!

Shortly after that Frances introduced a friend of hers to the family. His name was Bill Gianni. I was around eight or nine years old then. He was very wealthy worked at NASA, drove a fancy car, and had a big house! He really befriended the family and completely won my Mother's trust; bad mistake! Now you have to remember, I was a good girl, never got into trouble and was shy, skinny, ugly, and spent my time in the little patch of woods between the apartments and the school making mud patties and playing in the rain! I recently drove by that little patch of woods and it is still there!

He is the one who got me smoking cigarettes. He also continuously molested me for several years! He was fat and disgusting! I was so little I always had to be on top. I didn't know any better, I was too young to even understand! I will never understand what was in my Mother's head to even let this happen. How could she send me over there with him week after week after week? How could my childhood be taken away and nobody knew or cared? Answers to questions will never be answered. He kept me silent by getting me addicted to cigarettes and me being so young, not knowing right from wrong. This went on for about 2 years! Finally one day it just stopped. 40+ years later when I asked my mother about it; boy was I shocked! He told her that I come on to him and he felt guilty so he ended the relationship. By then Mother was old, frail, and Demetria had set in. I shouldn't have kept that secret so many years and asked her a long time ago! Should of...

This sexual abuse did leave its scars on me. I have a phobia about obese men and I have never been able to have sex with me on the top, plus a lifelong battle of anorexia! This also is the result in my strong desire to get people to eat healthy and stay in shape! Anorexia is a lifelong battle. Hell, even I didn't know that is what I suffered from for many years. I just thought that I hated food, I didn't connect the dots. As a matter of fact; it was when I saw the movie about Karen Carpenter's life that the light bulb went off inside my brain and that is when I realized I had a problem! A lifelong problem! **+++4**

17

Good memories

There were some good memories. On Saturdays, taking the bus downtown with my friend Mary Anne; going to Woolworth's, the library, being a big girl! And yes still playing in that small patch of trees making mad patties! And I can't forget the turtles! That was the craze baby turtles in a small bowl with a palm tree. Amazing I was a thumb sucker until I was in 4th grade, had lots of turtles and never got sick! That was the only pet I was allowed to have!

Every year there was a family reunion on my mother's side in Henderson, NC. What fun those family reunions were. It is funny. We would drive through Franklin, Virginia and the smell of the paper mill. It was almost an every year conversation about how bad it smelled and how we would never live there. I also remember the house that I call home now.

Moral of the story: never say never, it will bite you in the ass every time!

18

Roller Coaster Ride

Like I said I only had two friends growing up. Dana was several years older than I was. She was into things way before I should have been, but she was the only one that would give me the time of day, much less be a friend! I remember I would sneak out the bedroom window and we would sit on porch to my apartment building talking for hours! Dreaming about a better life! One time, she had a party, I was not allowed to go. That night I slipped out of the bedroom window as I had done so many times, only this time Mom and Harry came looking for me! The only time in my childhood I got into trouble, and I got a whipping! I didn't sneak out again!

Sometime after that, when I was in either the 4th or 5th grade, Alice Cooper came to the Hampton Coliseum. I didn't know who he was but I was allowed to go to the concert with my friend Dana. Alice Cooper was a no show, so everyone got sent home after several hours of his no show appearance. I never listened to him then and I never did afterwards. The no show and remembering the rowdy crowd was enough for me! To this day it amazes me why my Mother would let me go to such a concert. It totally blows my mind! What was she thinking?

This would be the beginning of a very long roller coaster ride! What a ride it has been! How I manage to survive this roller coaster is a miracle! Yes, I am living proof that miracles happens every day!

So in a very short period I went from making mud patties, to sexual abuse, then to an Alice Cooper!

One day shortly after the Alice Cooper concert I was helping my Mother with laundry. The last thing I remember was her yelling "get a spoon she's swelling her tongue!". The next thing I remember was being in the Hospital surrounded by all these people in white (back then all Doctors and nurses wore white), asking me "why did you do it?" I was completely clueless. I remember laying there for hours many be even days wondering; what in the hell were they talking about? Do what? Somebody tell me something, anything. I was being badgered to answer a question that I couldn't. No one would listen, I couldn't answer their questions, I didn't know the answer! Finally out of desperation I said "because Mother wouldn't let me visit Humphrey". Bingo they had an answer, they didn't care if it was a made up answer, and they just had an answer!

Many, many, many years would go by before I had the answer to what happened. I had an answer would be seizure. This is courtesy of one fantastic neurologist!

19

Drop And Run

Next thing I knew; Mother had packed me a small bag, I don't even remember stopping home when I got out of the hospital. We were headed to upstate N.Y. where she dropped me off at my father, Humphrey's house. It was a very fast drop and run. Life had bit me in the ass again!

Now Humphrey's house was quite a culture shock. Since him and my Mother had divorced when I was only one year old, I really did not know my father. I had met him only a few times! After divorcing my Mother, he married a woman named Alice. Alice was a tee total trip! It was just here recently that my sister Donna and I were talking about our visits with her (I only remember one). I must have really been young. I have always been a picky eater. This was inexcusable with Alice (since then I have learned that this is a heredity, several of my Grandchildren would inherit this trait)! She had a rule: if you didn't eat it for supper, you would eat it for breakfast. If you still didn't eat it for breakfast then you would get it for lunch, and so on...I remember going a very long time without eating on more than one occasion!

I do believe she is the number one reason for my fear of water and drowning! I was one of those kids that didn't like water in my eyes. Every household probably has a young child like that. She went to wash my hair and I was putting up a fuss about the water getting in my eyes and she grabbed my head and held it under that running bath water! Freaked me tee totally out! Never do that to a child! To this day, as an older woman, I am probably the only one who can drown in the shower! It doesn't matter how hard I hold my breath that water is going up my nose! Enough about Alice!

Back to being dropped off at Humphrey's house: At that time in his life, he had 4 boys. Plus he had a girlfriend living with him. Her name was Claire. Claire had 8 children, 7 were still at home! 11 children in that small 3 bedroom house! Here I was the baby girl and all of a sudden there were eleven! 100% culture shock!

Living with all these strangers was quite an experience in itself. There was Rhonda; she was older than me, Carol; who was the same age as me, Leanne who was younger than me, and ... Leanne needed anger management! There was one time, I don't remember how Carol and I pissed her off, but we did. The next thing we knew she was chasing us around the downstairs with a huge butcher knife. We locked ourselves in the bathroom but the door was made of slats and she busted it down! About that time Claire or Humphrey came home and saved the day!

What an amazing experience living with all these other children! One like no other. Little did I know it was preparing me for my future. I did get to experience some good things; I learned about the Catholic religion, I was in middle school and I took "shop" which back then girls did not do. I wanted a box with a lock on it, to keep all the kids out. I wanted to choke the instructor on several occasions, he wanted everything perfect and all I wanted was a box with a lock! By the end of the semester I had my small box with a lock. I have that box today; it is still one of my prize processions!

20

ADD

Humphrey liked to start projects but had a hard time finishing them. One winter, he was adding on to the house. We went all winter with one wall in kitchen being nothing but plastic. It was a cold winter too. That was the same year, the snow got so deep, we were jumping out of the second story window into the snow. Classic sigh of ADD. **+++5**

I didn't hear from my Mother at all. I remember talking to her on the phone one time. I guess this was her calgon take me away time. She was happy and content with my stepfather and half-brother Ricky. Many years later I asked her why she never called or why she never come and got me. It wasn't until after her death in 2007 that I would know the real reason. That reason would be: not being educated enough to understand the legal papers that the State of NY would eventually send her and...

21

Alcoholism

It was those middle school years that took me down the road with alcohol. I remember the first time I came home drunk, of course someone told on me! Humphrey came upstairs and he said "leave her alone, let her sleep it off". I slept if off alright and kept going back for more! So that is what I learned in middle school, how to drink beer and make a box!

It would be many years before scientist and doctors discovered the genetics of alcoholism. Studies have shown that a family history of alcoholism have a higher risk of developing a drinking problem. Some show as much as 50%. Our hereditary behaviors interact with our environment to form a basis of our decisions. Environmental factors that are particularly risky, who are genetically incline include: physical abuse, sexual abuse, witnessing violence, and peer pressure to name a few. **+++6**

22

Trying To Get Home

By the time I got to the beginning of 9th grade, it was like; o.k. I can't take this anymore; I'm out of here! I packed a few things in my backpack and as soon as I got off the bus at school, I hit the road. I hitch hiked from upstate N.Y. to Syracuse, N.Y. I called my drinking buddy, who had recently moved there and I stayed at his house for a few days. I had to get a game plan. I had to have time to think!

I came up with the game plan to hitchhike back to my Mother's house, I didn't care if she wanted me or not I was going! That day I managed to get my way through Syracuse and I was at the entrance to the highway, taking me South. A woman named Mrs. Hazard picked me up. She was so sweet to me. She asked me what my name was and I told her Frances Mayle. She took me to her house and I was in amazement! She had an indoor swimming pool, a microwave (I had never seen one of those), a nice car, and all these luxuries that I had never seen before! I slept like a baby all warm and cozy! Of course the whole time we talked she was prying information out of me. I was still on the naïve side. I woke up the next morning and she had called Mrs. Mayle (my sister; Donna's husband's Mother). Mrs. Mayle was more than happy to fill her in on who I was. I must have stayed with her for a couple days because she took me into town and bought me a coat. This was the first really nice coat I ever had. I cherished that coat for many years before it fell apart. The next thing was the call to Social Services. Into the foster care system I went!

23

Foster Care

I went to a temporary foster home for a couple of days. Then they placed me with a couple. He was in the Military and she was a stay at home mom. I want to say her name was Patsy. They had a teenage daughter and then a son in middle school. She was a professional foster Mother! In my room was two sets of bunkbeds, and then in another room she had more bunkbeds. Then of course her two children had a room to their own. We had our chore list: 3 times a week each of us would be given a room to clean and it had to pass the white glove test! I laugh now because boy did I fail those tests. The only room I seemed to get right was the living room and that was because the only time it was used was when a social worker came.

One time I was assigned the entrance way. Now really, who can screw up cleaning an entrance hallway? I can! I put so much wax on the floor; it had to be striped all the way down. That was the first and last time I ever used wax! Another one was the upstairs bathroom (which we were not supposed to use); heaven forbid I had streaks on the mirror!

She was kind enough to buy our cigarettes at the commissary. You have to remember times were different back then. Everybody smoked! We had our own smoking area outside at one particular corner of the house. I remember freezing our ass off but that was our get together for all of us foster kids. A time when we could all share our horror stories and laugh!

So here I went from having no rules to being in the military. A huge kick in the ass! It didn't take long and I was out of there.

Humphrey actually picked me up and took me back to his house. We got back and Claire and all her kids were gone! Humphrey politely told me that the reason he picked me up. He needed me to take care of the boys! He went to work the next day, and I was hitchhiking again. I was going back to the foster home!

I ended up going back to the temporary foster home and then to a new one in small town of N.Y. This one was different. This time I was the only foster child, and they had a daughter my age; if I remember right her name was Betty. They were catholic also so they had a lot of children.

It was in that home that I tried some new experiences, ice skating was one. Back then all ice skates were single bladed. No matter how hard I tried, I could not stand up without my ankles giving way. After numerous attempts, I figured I wasn't meant for me to ice skate. Now in my adult years, I get much enjoyment out of watching figure ice skating. To me, it is the best part of the Olympics'!

Another thing I tried was tennis. Another attempt at something I couldn't do. I gave it my best shot though. For some reason the racket just couldn't find the damn ball! For days they tried to teach me and for days the ball went right past the racket. I didn't realize it back then but my hand eye coordination sucks! I was not gifted in that department at all!

This is the time I had my first boyfriend, I was in 9th grade. I also met my third close friend, Evelyn. I was happier there, in that small town then I had been in years! Little did I know that the state of New York had other plans. My life was getting ready to go through more drastic changes. Couldn't I just get a break and be happy? No, that wasn't allowed!

24

The Big Apple

Towards the end of 9th grade, I was informed by my social worker that I was going to live with my sister Frances in Brooklyn, N.Y. Sometime while in foster care she had moved to N.Y. in their jurisdiction. Bags packed and boom I was gone off to Brooklyn, leaving the small town life and friends that I had grown to love. My boyfriend and I did try to keep a long distance relationship. In fact, I went to his prom with him that year. The only prom, I would ever go to.

Now, let me explain Frances, if I can. She was a flower child. A product of the 60's who never left the 60's! She was into the drugs, burning bras, rock n roll music; she also had a huge heart, no doubt about that! She met Rocky who at one time was the manager of a band. They had two children.

Moving from small towns to NYC was a trip in itself! Talk about culture shock, I was in it as far as you could go! Plus add to fact; I was living with strangers again. Frances was 11 years older than me. It is not like we were close. She taught me some pretty amazing life lessons back then and then again later in my years.

Since music was Frances' life it turned into my life. I might have been on 15 years old but I was about reach for the stars and never knew it was coming.

We lived in a small house behind a larger house in the Italian section of Brooklyn. The summer was great, free concerts in Central Park, blocks parties. These were for real block parties! The whole block would be blocked off and everyone would cook, there was music and dancing, everyone having a grand time!

Since we lived in a safe neighborhood, I was quickly taught how to go to the coffee shop to buy fresh ground coffee. Oh, the smell of it walking back home. I'll never forget that smell. It smelled so good and I wasn't a coffee drinker.

This is the time in my life that I learned about old movies. I fell in love with them and I still love them to this day! I will even watch the old silent ones, I love them all. I found my favorite actor Jimmy Stewart and of course Betty Davis. I love them all; James Cagney, Humphrey Bogart, Lauren Bacall, the list can go on and on. Watch them sometime!

25

Treasures

What may appear as trash to you, maybe your child's treasurers!

It was during my time living with Frances that I was able to go home for the first time. What a life shocker that was! I expected to have all of my life's treasurer's pack away for me, after all I wasn't given the opportunity to pack them. She had saved me one small box. I was devastated! I asked her where my things were and she told me "I gave them to a little girl that needed them." What in the hell was she talking about, I needed them! They were mine!

What makes people hoard food? These are the people who at one time in their life have been without food!

This act would lead to a lifetime act of trying to recover what was lost. Giving away my treasures brock my heart! My treasures were my baby dolls and the clothes that were handmade for them, my easy bake oven, my records, my pictures from the magazines hanging on the wall. My things.

This one act, lead to collecting baby dolls for the next thirty years. Not just any doll but very specific dolls all related to the era of my childhood. I was one of the fortunate ones. It was probably twenty years ago that I realized why I was collecting them. I was able to stop once I realized the reason why. I turned into a collector of books, antiques, and enamelware.

Which by the way, will be on my Esty.com shop by the late winter early spring of 2017. Yes, I am actually downsizing!

One of my sisters was not so lucky. She was traumatized by losing her treasures! She turned into a hoarder. Is she able to control herself? No.

Many people wonder "What makes a person a hoarder". The answer is quite simple. Throw away your child's treasurers! As a parent you have no idea what is a treasurer to your child. It can be rocks, old nails, plastic bottles, paperclips, magazines', books, dolls, pictures, you name it. The sky is the limit in a child's eye. You take away all of their "treasures" and they are left filling empty. They will forever try and recover that pebble, doll, record, etc. It took me around 30 years to figure out, why I collected all the things that I have. I was trying to get my childhood back! +++7

26

Adventures Continue

Frances taught me how to ride the subway. She took me to several places such a St. Patrick's Cathedral, Times Square, the Staten Island Ferry to ride it across and back to view the Statue of Liberty, and of course to Chinatown to eat at the famous (from the old movies) 21 restaurant!

Then school started. It was all downhill from there! Of course, it was very difficult for me to make friends, plus these kids were different. A lot different! I remember being in the restroom one time and one of the girls was complaining to another girl that she didn't have time to put on her makeup. I looked at her and she had eyeliner on, etc... and I was standing wondering what in the hell she talking about, she had makeup on! The class sizes were so big and everybody was always in a hurry. I also had to walk my niece Kyle to Elementary school since she just started kindergarten. I don't remember how far away the Elementary School was from Brooklyn High, it couldn't have been that far.

Then things took a turn for the worst. Frances had made some friends, there was John, Lenny and some I don't remember their name. Looking back at it, John was by far the worst influence. So Frances started partying more and more, getting more undependable. I had to quit school to take care of my two nieces. They were too young, I had no choice and it is a choice that I would do all over again.

27

Birthday Present

I did get my freedom occasionally. I was befriended by a gentleman, who Frances had met. She had given him her phone number. Since I was the one home taking care of the kids while Rocky worked, I was the one answering the phone when this smooth talking gentleman would call. He talked me into meeting him and talked me into quite a bit of other things I am not proud of and for over 40 years secret. He would video tape our sex, telling me it was for his study or book or whatever excuse he made. He also pimped me out to another man on several occasions. I think to me, it was just the fact that I was getting attention. Evidently, the attention was something that I was craving and very much lacking. He was such a smooth talker and very believable for someone just at the ripe age of 15.

I got pregnant right about the time of my 16th birthday. I told him I was pregnant and he said we needed to "take care of it". I didn't like what he was suggesting, so I never talked to him again.

In the meantime, when Frances found out I was pregnant; I remember her exact words "how could you do this to me?" I remember thinking "Do this to her, I am the one pregnant!" Right after that, I had another reality check: I came home and Rocky had taken the girls and left. I had no idea where they had gone, and why didn't he take me with them? Answers to questions I will never know.

So that left me in NYC, completely alone! Frances went to live with John, if I remember correctly, she didn't invite me to live with them, and I was clueless on what to do or where to go.

28

Twin Towers

I don't remember exactly how but I ended up running into a nice young man; Richard who let me move in with him, in Manhattan. This apartment was a bachelor's paradise, it was right around the corner from the twin towers and right there by the Staten Island Ferry. There were 4 gentlemen who all shared this huge apartment which extended several floors, they all had good paying jobs and I really enjoyed living with them. At night, after Wall Street closed, we would take the monkeys out to play in the trees by the Staten Island Ferry. We were in a world by ourselves after office hours, a nice piece of paradise!

This would be my first experience in the world of animals. An experience that has lasted a life time. Why, because animals accept you for who you are!

I got my first job as a waitress, but that didn't last long. The owners wanted to pay me with their used clothing not a paycheck! Then reality set in, as I was really starting to show that I was pregnant. Courtland was an architect that worked in Philadelphia. He really took me under his wing. He ran across the article in the paper about my unborn child's Father. That article I tried to find for the rest of my life and haven't found it yet. He was the one that contacted my mother to see if she would take me in. He bought me a Greyhound Bus ticket and back to Virginia I would go! We stayed in contact for a couple of years. He got my back pay from the waitress job and mailed it to me. He took me on vacation with him to Sanibel Island in FL, when my son was a little under a year old. I often wonder how he is doing. I have tried several times to look him up and thank him for saving mine and my son's life but I don't even know how to correctly spell his name, so I have had a difficult time.

The Greyhound bus trip, back home to Virginia was fun! I had a black cat; "Sabbath" named after the Sabbath day not the rock group. Anyway, at that time animals were not allowed on the bus, it might even still be a rule (except for the handicap). I was not about to leave Sabbath, so I went out and we bought some secondhand baby clothing and I dressed him and wrapped him in the blankets like he was a baby. It worked, although I did almost get busted with him a couple of times with his meows.

29

Back Home

I finally got back home! I was so excited! Home, home, home. But it wasn't home. I thought that I was going to come home to a mother with loving arms and support for what I had be through. That was not the case. They had moved from the old apartment into a new apartment in the same apartment complex but in a newer section. There were four apartments downstairs and four upstairs. They had managed to get my Granny, my Aunt Shirley, and her all in the same building! This made it a lot easier for Mother since they didn't own a car and relied on her. Remember, this was nothing new for Mother. She was always the caregiver for her siblings all during her younger years. Diabetics ran strong in her blood line and several of her siblings had already passed away from complications relating to the "uncontrollable diabetics" that they suffered from. Thank goodness for modern science and health care.

Me coming back home, just meant she had one more person for her to take of. Not having medical insurance, she enlisted the aid of Catholic Charities. I was talked into putting the baby up for adoption when it was born. Now, you have to remember, I didn't even start to show that I was pregnant until in my sixth month. So, all of this happened in a rather short period of time. So here she was; with the added burden of my doctor appointments and my appointments with Catholic charities plus taking care of Granny, Aunt Shirley, my half-brother Ricky, Harry and working! She must have had too much extra stress.

Then I had news for all of them, I had decided not to put the baby up for adoption, much to the dismay from others. Having that baby grow and move inside of me was a wonderful experience. It was something that was mine, and I wanted to keep it! The night I went into labor, Mother and Aunt Shirley took me the hospital. When I got out of the car my water broke. Once I was in the hospital, they put me in a maternity ward, it was a large room with many beds. I was the only one there. They never gave my anything for the pains and I was left completely alone. Finally, a nurse showed back up and I was pushing. I was told to blow not push. Blow what in the hell was she talking about? Nobody ever explained or went over with me what labor and delivery was, I was clueless. The doctor came in and the baby's head was already coming out, so the rest of delivery went really fast.

30

Motherhood

I came home with my beautiful baby boy! I wasn't prepared for Motherhood at all, I was only 16 and all though I had been though a lot, I was still naive about a lot. I had never taken care of a baby! Mother showed my some tricks of the trade and that was it. I would get no help from her, he was mine and she really didn't want any part of it. Somewhere in the back of my mind, I think I truly believed that Daniel; my son, would make a huge difference in our relationship. To be honest, I think it pushed her away even further.

I used the name Daniel from my favorite bible story: Daniel and the Lions Den. I am sure that it also played into the factor; that Elton John's song "Daniel" was released in 1973. By giving him a strong name to me, that was my gift to him. A strong name to me meant; that he would be destined to do great things. I felt so strongly about this that all three of my sons were given strong biblical names. +++8

I got a job right up the road at the local theater. The same one that I went to in my younger years. It was great having a job and money! What I didn't realize is, I had to pay a babysitter. I ended up getting the wife of one of my cousins to babysit, and fortunately she didn't charge an arm and a leg. Going to work was one of the best things that I could have done. I was able to buy Daniel's clothes, take him to get his picture taken, all the things I thought a Mother should do. I also met friends and even got a boyfriend! I was actually was enjoying life!

31

Short Lived

This was short lived. All of a sudden out of the blue, Mother told me, they got a two bedroom apartment in the other end of Town. Two bedrooms, one for her and Harry and the other for Ricky. Aunt Shirley was moving to a high rise in Downtown, Granny was moving to a senior community close, to where Mother got her apartment. There was no talk or mention where I and my baby were moving to. Total shock again!

This is where I would like to thank Nancy, for she was our lifesaver. I was dating her best friend's brother Larry. It was agreed that Larry and I would move in together. We just had to find somewhere. Nancy drove me around looking for someplace that was in close proximity to her house and her best friend's Toni's house. We finally ran across a rental house that fit. Little did I know, that Larry had plans to have his two children; Marley and Little Larry live with us also. So all of a sudden I was a Mother of three, had to cook, clean, etc... I was living my Mother's past life!

I'll never forget, one day I cooked a ham. Now I had never had to cook, didn't know how, and if it had not have been for the couple short cooking lessons in my very much younger days of being a Brownie (that is a younger version of being a Girl Scout), I wouldn't know what a measuring cup was! So I spent all day preparing this meal, we sat down to eat and we I must have done something wrong, for it was tough and we didn't have the correct knife to cut it. Larry got so mad he was cursing, ranting, and raving about my cooking. It ended with the dog having a feast! Needless to say this relationship was short lived.

The whole relationship between Larry and me was bad. At the ripe old age of 17, he taught me the world of going to bars. Something I had never experience before except for of course "The Bloody Bucket" from my childhood. Since he was known at these bars no one ever bothered to check my ID and the drinking age then was 21 and here I was just 17! I hadn't drunk since my early years at Humphrey's house.

Mother did help me get my first apartment when I was just 17. She convinced the apartment manager to rent me the apartment. She did take me to get groceries once in a while but for the main part, I was on my own. It was this time in my life where I learned how to make one Pepsi last all day, and other real money saving tricks that I still use today.

Since all the bars that Larry had introduced me to were right there. I started to take advantage of one that was within walking distance. That is where I found the world of military men. I was so attracted to them, everything about them, their build, their life style, their cars, and their uniforms. I could spot one in an instance. I got a boyfriend named; Greg. We were perfect for each other, so I thought. There was only one big catch, he was married! The three of us: Greg, his wife and I, tried to make a go of it. Greg wanted both of us. After much dismay, I had to let him go, I wasn't any good at sharing and neither was she.

32

Neighbors

I met some of my neighbors. One of them was Barb and Bill. I met them when I went over to offer apologies for stealing their Sunday paper. I told them that "it would sit there all day, and so I would come over and get it, read it, and put it back". They became really close friends of mine for many years to come.

33

Married Life

Then I met Jim. Jim was fun, he taught me how to drive and before long I was drag racing his Ranchero (that's a car with a pickup truck rear end), and winning! I found it completely satisfying to drag race and win! It was such an adrenaline rush! Within three months of us meeting, we got married!

Married life was great! We bought a house near Buckroe, I got a job at Arby's. Things were really headed in the right direction. The bars were a thing of the past. We were happy as a family. You know the old saying don't count your chickens before they hatch. That is the perfect saying for this situation. I still had not learned about birth control, so of course I got pregnant right away. This wasn't a bad thing, I was married, had a good husband, a home, a job that I liked. Everything was going in the right direction. It was about time, it had been a long 19 years and long overdue.

When I was pregnant I worked right up until a couple of days before I had him and went back to work two weeks after I had him. I cannot understand the women today, having to take so much time off of work. But then again, we are in a different world then today's world. Life was still great! I totally enjoyed being a wife and Mother. Then it happened. He got orders and was moving to England! It was agreed, he would go ahead of me and "secure housing" then send for me and my children. Great game plan, so I thought. So he left, the military came and packed up all of our household belongings. It would be years before I would know that they didn't pack up the shed or the attic. All of that stuff was left behind. I would never know, why he never sent for us, or why it took so long to "secure housing", questions in my life that will never be answered.

34

Bouncing

The kids and I lived here there and everywhere. From Ohio with his parents then back to Suffolk with my sister, no place to call home once again. In Suffolk, I got a job as a waitress. I got our own apartment and had moved on with my life. By then a year had passed since Jim was going to "secure housing" and send for us. I had given up on that idea. I have never figured out what was so hard about securing housing. I would have taken anything even a one bedroom apartment. I remember lying in bed wondering why it was taking so long. After a year, I had completely given up.

One time during that year, I needed a new vacuum cleaner. It was not and could not fit into the budget. So, I used Jim's Mother and took the boys there for two weeks while I worked two full time jobs so I could buy one. I was so proud of myself! I took that money and made the trip to Hampton and went to the commissary and picked out my brand new Eureka vacuum cleaner. I cherished that vacuum cleaner for many years to come for I knew how hard I had to work to purchase it.

Then I got involved with the wrong friends or should I say boyfriend and his friends. Drinking and partying became a way of life. It wasn't a good life either. Booze will grab you by the balls and pull you right down to the pits of hell!

35

Gypsy Life

Then out of the blue I met Bill Ford. He painted water towers for
a living. He was a good man, hardworking and always looking
out for the best interest of my children. So on the road with him
we went. It was a fantastic time. We traveled to so many places
and we saw so much. In the winter we would be south where it
was warm, in the summer we would be up north. It was so
much fun, I loved it! Drinking was a thing of the past, at least
for a little while.

36

Reality Check

Then we had to do a reality check. The gypsy life could be no more, no more living in Motels, no more traveling, the end. Daniel had to go to school. We rented a house in North Little Rock, Arkansas. At first things were great, he was home every night, I went back to school and got my G.E.D. Daniel was in a private Christian school. Life was good. Then his jobs started getting further away. He could not make it home every day. It had turned into just a weekend thing. To comfort myself, I started drinking again. Remember the pits of hell? It didn't take any time to get there!

Times did get a little tough financially, while living with Bill. He made good money and I did not handle the bills but I knew it was tough. A young man came to work for the same company Bill worked for. They immediately made friends. The next thing I knew I was off to upstate NY to pick up his wife and children. I didn't think twice about driving from Arkansas all the way to upstate NY.

It was also during this same period that I had yet another life shocker! We had a house full with two families living together. Two men, two women, and five young children in a two bedroom house! One day, I came home and Bill had cooked dinner. We were sitting around the table saying grace and started to eat. I thought that "chicken" looks mighty different, then it tasted different. Much to my surprise when I asked, the answer I was not what I was prepared for; it was our pet rabbit! I do not think me or my boys ate dinner that night!

Bill wasn't even out the picture yet when I found Falcon. He was my next partner in life. Bill became a thing of the past. Long gone but will never be forgotten. By then, I was working at another Arby's and was being trained as Manager. Falcon became the live in Nanny. By day he was my nanny and at night my drinking buddy.

It was training as Manager, that I had my first up close and personal tornado experience. I was working, the District Manager was there also. We had a tornado warning! We were in tornado alley so this was not unusual. We were both out back smoking a cigarette and boom it was there! We watched it, touch down, and ripped off the Walmart roof! I was so hypnotized by the whole experience, I don't think I ever moved. To this day, I still refer to it as an amazing experience! Stupid for standing that close and watching it but an experience that is forever a thriller!

I got promoted to General Manager and moving to Hot Springs, Ark. A move that would later be a bad move. Now, you have to remember that being a dedicated hard worker was instilled in me during my younger years. This was my normal. I give everything that I do, 110%, not matter how hard it is, and how many hours I work. I was taught it was the way of life.

Falcon was not a good fit for me that is putting it lightly. He was a good guy, he took really good care of the boys and tried to take good care of me. It is just we were too much alike. We both liked to party, so of course life was one big party after I got off work! It didn't take long for it to take its toll on me. I left him and moved back to Virginia in 1982. We tried to keep up with each other but over time we lost each other.

37

Back To Virginia

I moved in with my Mother briefly. Larry came back into the picture very quickly and we moved in together. This was also very short lived. It didn't work the first time, what made me think it would work the second? I took a job as General Manager of Arby's again. I got my own apartment in the same complex that I had lived in before my first marriage. Hooked up with my old friends Bill and Barb and continued down life's journey.

Arby's didn't work out. Different values, mine was loyalty to the store and to my customers. The owner want me to be loyal to coming to a meeting when my fryers were broken and I was trying to get them working. So we didn't see eye to eye. Needless to say I said take this job and shove it!

It didn't take me long to find my best friends Bill and Barb. I went to work for Bill, he had started his own construction company. I found that I like remodeling, taking something old and disgusting and turning it into something beautiful! I had found my niece. It was hard work but I was use to that. I worked for him for several years working my up the ladder to foreman. The last job before he closed his company and went to work for the federal government full time, was a house in one of the wealthiest parts of town. Talk about a rags to riches ending!

With him closing his company, I had too much time on my hands. Where did I turn? Partying of course, what else did I know? I couldn't get a job in another construction company, I was only 98 pounds dripping wet, it didn't matter what kind of reference Bill wrote. Back then, it just wasn't heard of.

I lost my apartment and moved in with Bill and Barb. During the day while both of them worked I would do small repairs on their house and have dinner ready when they got home. This was hard for Barb to handle because she was used to doing; all the cooking and cleaning. Barb was a nightly drinker and Bill was a nightly smoker, so of course I was right there smoking and drinking with them. It was party hardy on the weekends! Of course this was unacceptable behavior for my relatives.

38

Wayward Again

A few months or really I don't remember how long I had been living with them but my Mother came knocking on the door and said 'she came to get Daniel". So she took him, I have no clue as to why all of a sudden it was important to raise him. She had never offered a hand before, why now? Family rumors get started and when one person tells another person, then another, the story always comes out different. Maybe it was Barb who called her, maybe not, who knows.

Both of sons were big Momma boys. They were with me constantly and my youngest still slept with me every night. After Mother took Daniel, that was it for me. I started hitting the drinking bad, trying to wash my blues away, damn country songs!

The next thing I knew, my sister was coming after Benjamin. That hit me really hard. I went hog wild! Talk about life in the fast lane. Life became on huge party and there was no looking back! Looking back at it now, I was doing all the things that I had been accused of my whole life! I was living out my teenage years and more.

I have no clue how long this lasted, I would have to get my records out and right now that is not high on my priority list. I could go into a long tell about just this part of my life but I'll leave it alone for now.

After a while, I ended up back at my old stomping grounds with Larry. I met a man named Don. I ended up moving in with him, I could not handle the conditions he lived in so we got an apartment and started from scratch. We had become the best of friends. All of a sudden one morning I woke up and said "what in the hell are you doing". That was it, my party days stopped just like that, in an instance. No withdraws, no headaches, no meds, no nothing. At that time, little 98 pound me was drinking a case of beer a day and boom I just quit! Just like that! I missed my children!

39

Wake Up Call

I had to get my life together and I had to do it fast. Never underestimate the power of a willful individual, for we have super powers that are unmatched by any other. By then, Mother was tired of raising my son. She immediately gave him back. No questions asked. Getting Ben back was another story. So I married Don, just to look good and stable so I could get my son back. It was a quick wedding, and I wore a red dress. Never get married in a red dress, it is an old folk tale that it brings bad luck to the marriage. This would become a reality. We had not been friends long enough to really know each other, plus the whole time we were drinking buddies, which played a whole different role.

Somewhere right about the time we got married, I got pregnant again. It was after Joshua was born, before I was able to get Benjamin back. By then, I think too much time had passed, he held too many grudges. He also wasn't too fond of the fact that he had a baby brother. Maybe it was too much change at one time. Maybe he felt like I had abandoned him, maybe, maybe, maybe.

Bringing Don into my life brought more challenges than I was aware of. I was working as the General Manager of Shoney's at the time. Don's father: Captain (that was his nickname) would come into Shoney's and that is where we formed a close relationship.

We had wonderful talks during his visits as I worked. He had a heart attack and passed away that winter. I remember everyone was so worried about me because by then, I was far along in my pregnancy.

40

Ghosts In The Attic

A few months later, we were moving into the house that Don grew up in as a child. I was about to learn the hard way, it was a wrong thing to do. I didn't know, that it would bring Don's childhood ghosts that he had not dealt with to the surface. There were a lot of ghost! All of a sudden, I had to deal with all the bad things that were done to him as a child. He had held inside of him all those years.

He did have it rough as a child. I have to admit that. He had an evil stepmother. He was getting punished severely on a daily basis because he couldn't read. These beatings and punishments' that he went through, he locked away in his mind. They did not come out again until we moved back into his childhood home. He would sit in the office behind closed doors for hours. Never wanting to be disturbed. The whole time he was hiding in the office, I believe he was reliving his childhood. The physical abuse that I went through would leave scars and wounds both physical and mental.

The abuse got so bad! I did leave and went to a shelter for battered women. It didn't take him long to convince me: he was going to change. I should give him a second chance. He quit drinking, attended AA meetings and I thought he was headed down the right road. During some of this time, I was attending college full time, worked part time and also took care of his aging Grandmother. Looking back at it, I wonder how I managed to do everything, plus had three children!

We ended up, opening our own business. This went good at the beginning. He made friends with the wrong crowd and his drinking started back again. He tried to take me down the same road but I was strong and wouldn't let him. I went to a lawyer. He was drunk at our business and this was interfering with our business. He was chasing the customers away! I was politely informed by the lawyer, there wasn't a damn thing I could do about it. "He owned 50% of it." I had all that I could take. I closed the doors!

41

Hinshaw Mansion

Once again, he tried to turn me into his drinking buddy again. It didn't work. When it didn't work he became more and more violent. I knew I had to protect me and my children but how? The answer became, what is still referred to as the "hinshaw mansion". It was a far cry from a mansion: no heat, run down, but I was able to keep the children in the same school and it was economy available.

What a first year that was! I made sure the boys had heat in their room and every morning I would get up way before them. I would get the fireplace going to warm the kitchen and living room, somewhat. I would wake up in the morning and my glass of water that I took to my bedroom with me had frozen into ice! I always kept my bedroom closed off to conserve what little bit of heat the fireplace would put out. This was an extremely hard winter for me. Don had followed me and I couldn't make him move out. I sank deeper and deeper.

42

Diagnosis

I was trying to deal with living in such a raggedy house and an abusive husband. It was also the time my youngest son was being tested. He was just two years old but I could tell something wasn't quite right. I had raised enough children, I knew. They came back with a diagnosis of mildly mentally retarded. What in the hell did that mean? This was my child, they were talking about!

Over the course of a few years, Joshua's diagnoses would change. Each time: they had learned more about the brain and how it works. I even went so far as to have his genes tested but I was ahead of the doctors on that one. I knew it was something heredity but they couldn't pin point it. Finally at the age of twelve, I had him tested by the top neurologist in the state of Virginia. That would be his last diagnoses but a more accurate one. By then, he had given up on the doctors and I do not blame him.

43

Hero Or Not

At the time of this testing and trying to get Don out, there was a gentleman. He rented the garage apartment of the "hinshaw mansion". It was New Year's Eve night, and I had just come back from Nancy's house, when, we really talked for the first time. That night, we stayed up all night just talking! It was exactly a week later, January 7, I couldn't resist anymore. He was every girl's dream, muscular, good looking, hardworking, and seemed to genuinely care. It took him no time to get Don out of the house, he was my hero or was he?

44

Closing The Chapter

To completely close the chapter on Don, let me tell you the rest of the story (As Paul Harvey would say). As I said earlier, Don and I were close friends. We did not make a good husband and wife team! I couldn't deal with all the ghosts in his closet or his drinking. We remained close friends for years to come, until his death. There is or probably never will be anyone, who knew or knows the real me. We continued to talk for hours throughout his life, each one telling our deepest secrets. There was also two times after we divorced that he came to live with me again. One of those times is in the house I live in today, after his open heart surgery. That's what best friends are for. Lasting relationships share and remember your life experiences. They accept you for who you are.

45

Adversity

All through life we have adversity. Adversity is a condition of hardship and suffering involving heartaches, disappointments, trials, and anguish. We make so many decisions throughout our life. The one thing we never choose is adversity. It would be great if we could avoid these times but we cannot.

When adversity happens you have several choices on how to handle it. You can choose to nurture your hurt and anger and waste your life or you can learn and grow from the experience. If you believe in a higher power, this is a perfect time to grow your relationship with your higher power. This is an excellent opportunity to develop some excellent qualities such as; patience, unshakeable faith, and courage.

We may not have a choice regarding adversity but we do have a choice on how to respond. Do not live your life in rebellion and waste your life, use this time to grow!

46

No One Is Perfect

You see, no one is perfect. You have to accept people for who they are. Something that appears to be getting harder and harder for people to do. Everyone has flaws, you have to decide if you can accept those flaws or not. I like what Sally Field said in the movie Forrest Gump "life is like a box of chocolates, you never know what you are going to get."

47

Continue Learning

Internet Sites:

+++1: http://.www.history.com/topics/baby-boomers

+++2: https://ghr.nlm.nih.gov/primer#inheritance

+++3: https://www.nimh.nih.gov/health/topics/bipolar-disorder/index.shtml

       http://www.mayoclinic.org/conditions/depression/basics/definition/con-20032977

       https://blog.kinstantly.com/kids-with-anxiety/

+++4: https://www.eatingdisorderhope.com/information/anorexia

+++5: https://www.add.org/

+++6: http://.www.addictioncenter.com/alcohol/genetics-of-alcoholism/

+++7: https://www.psychiatry.org/patients-families/hoarding-disorder/what-is-hoarding-disorder

+++8: http://lifehopeandtruth.com/prophecy/understanding-the-book-of-daniel/daniel-6/

       http://www.aboutbibleprophecy.com/p129.htm

       https://gotquestions.org/life-Joshua.html

(A BETTER UNDERSTANDING OF LIFES JOURNEYS in black and white)

Copyright © 2016 by Deborah Jeter

ISBN -13: 978-0692822067

ISBN-10: 0692822062

www.ingramcontent.com/pod-product-compliance
Lightning Source LLC
Chambersburg PA
CBHW020507030426
42337CB00011B/261